WORDS
of
PEACE
and
WELCOME

Register This New Book

Benefits of Registering*

- ✓ FREE **replacements** of lost or damaged books

- ✓ FREE **audiobook** – *Pilgrim's Progress*, audiobook edition

- ✓ FREE information about new titles and other **freebies**

www.anekopress.com/new-book-registration

*See our website for requirements and limitations.

WORDS
of
PEACE
and
WELCOME

**62 Days of Encouragement and
Inspiration for Christian Pilgrims**

HORATIUS BONAR

We enjoy hearing from our readers. Please contact us at www.anekopress.com/questions-comments with any questions, comments, or suggestions.

Words of Peace and Welcome

© 2024 by Aneko Press

All rights reserved. First edition 1923.

Revisions copyright 1860.

Cover Designer: J. Martin

Editor: C. Miskimen

Aneko Press

www.anekopress.com

Aneko Press, Life Sentence Publishing, and our logos are trademarks of

Life Sentence Publishing, Inc.
203 E. Birch Street
P.O. Box 652
Abbotsford, WI 54405

RELIGION / Christian Living / Inspirational

Paperback ISBN: 979-8-88936-342-2

eBook ISBN: 979-8-88936-343-9

10   9   8   7   6   5   4   3   2   1

Available where books are sold

Contents

The Quickening Spirit

And the Spirit of God moved
upon the face of the waters.
– Genesis 1:2

It had just been said *darkness was upon the face of the deep* or abyss (Genesis 1:2). Here it is said the Spirit moved upon, or brooded over, the face of the waters, showing us that the abyss was a watery waste of utter gloom.

Into this region of deep darkness, the Holy Spirit came, taking possession of it and filling it with His quickening power. For all quickening is from Him. He is the infinite, the almighty giver of life. As such, He showed Himself when coming down to brood over the lifeless earth. As such, He shows Himself when He comes down to brood over and fill with His life-breathing presence the dead soul of man.

There was nothing lovely on the earth to attract Him; yet He came. There was nothing fair or fragrant or loveable or holy to bring Him; yet He came. There was no trace of life below to form a magnetic power by which the life from above might be drawn down; yet He came. There was no sound or voice of the living to invite His coming or bid Him welcome when He arrived; yet He came. And like this, He comes still. Even though uninvited and unwelcomed, even though grieved and resisted; yet He comes! In the sovereignty of His power and of His grace He comes! If it were otherwise, where would the sinner's hope be?

He is the *free Spirit* (Psalm 51:12), and as such, is free to come to whomsoever He will. No amount of evil in us can hinder Him.

Day 2

God's Joy in His Works

*God saw every thing that he had made,
and, behold, it was very good.*
– Genesis 1:31

S uch is the joy of God! He *shall rejoice in His works* (Psalm 104:31). These were just *parts of His ways* (Job 26:14), the first scene in the unfolding of His wondrous purpose; yet it is very glorious, and in it He is well pleased. Each day's work was good, all things above and beneath; the heaven with its stars; the earth with its flowers, gems, hills, seas, and streams; man and beast and fowl; all were good.

How deep the interest that He takes in all that He has made! Each atom is His own, and each atom comes under His eye. It is not only the hairs of our head that are numbered nor the sparrow that He notices nor the lily of the field that He paints; but the very dust of the ground, the sand of the desert, the pebble on the ocean beach. All these are owned and cared for by

Him. How truly has this earth been called His "well-beloved world!"

This is the God in whom *we live, and move, and have our being* (Acts 17:28)! How deep His love! What will it not do for us in all things great and small! He cares for our earth and for us, its dwellers! His delight is to bless, and what amount of blessing will He count too great to bestow on those for whom He has already given His Son! Let us trust Him in everything. He will not fail us. He will do us good and not evil, abundantly, all the days of our lives.

Day 3

Security in the Evil Day

*And the L*ORD *shut him in.*
– Genesis 7:16

Then was he safe indeed! No peril could reach him, no enemy could find access, no sudden misfortune could surprise him. He was as safe in the midst of the rolling waters as was Enoch in the presence of that Lord to whom he was caught up that he might be taken away from the evil to come (Genesis 5:24).

He who shut Noah in, by that very act, shut out all evil. He shut out the flood, He shut out the storm, He shut out death. He gave a pledge to His faithful servant that all would be well. Above, there was darkness; beneath, the tossing wave; around, the moaning wind; far off and near, the cries of dying multitudes; yet Noah was secure. Jehovah had shut him in. Jehovah kept watch.

It is Jehovah who "shuts in" His Noahs, along with their families, in the day of evil. He has His rooms provided for them. He leads them into these when danger threatens. He secures them against enemies; He Himself stands sentinel at the gate.

In stormy times, let us call to mind this security. The name of the Lord is our strong tower; let us run into it and be safe (Proverbs 18:10). He calls us to enter, and He shuts us in. He keeps watch outside though the whole world, like a mighty flood, rise against us as if to overflow and overwhelm. He who shuts us in will keep us. We will not be moved. Jesus is our ark, and He who shuts us in is the Father.

Day 4

Light in Darkness

I do set my bow in the cloud.
– Genesis 9:13

It was out of the cloud that the deluge came, yet it is upon it that the bow is set! The cloud is a thing of darkness, yet God chooses it for the place where He bends the arch of light! It is on this mass of overhanging gloom that He spreads out, in all its sevenfold richness, the beauty of His wondrous light.

This is the way of our God. He knows that we need the cloud and that a bright sky without a speck or shadow would not help us in our passage to the kingdom. Therefore, He draws the cloud above us, not once in a lifetime, but many times. But lest the gloom should appall us, He braids that cloud with sunshine. He makes it the object that shines to our eye with the very fairest hues of heaven.

It is not merely light after the darkness has fled away. That we will one day know. How fully! But it is light in darkness; light beaming out of, produced by that darkness! Water from the rock; wells from the sand; light from the very cloud that darkens; life in the very midst of death! This is the marvel. This is the joy. Peace in trouble, gladness in sorrow; peace and gladness produced by the very tribulation itself. Peace and gladness that nothing but that tribulation could have produced! Such is the deep love of God, and such is the way in which He makes all things work together for good to us.

Our Everlasting Rock

Who is a rock, save our God?
– 2 Samuel 22:32

Yes, who is a rock, except He? Shelter, shadow, fortress, shield, and hiding place – all in Him! Jehovah, God of heaven and earth, the God who so loved the world as to give His only begotten Son – He is our Rock!

What shall we then say? If God be for us, who can be against us? (Romans 8:31). If He is our Rock, who can harm us? What storm of the ocean can overthrow us when established on this Rock, or what sun of the desert can scorch us when seated under the shadow of the Great Rock in the weary land?

Let us trust and not be afraid. Let us be without anxiety. Let us not forecast evil or trouble ourselves about the future. All is well. Who is a rock except our God? We have good reason to be calm and peaceful. We have a good right to be steadfast and unmovable.

It is not we that have made the Rock nor placed it where it is. It is Jehovah Himself, and He has done it for us.

It is on this Rock that the Holy Spirit places us when He draws us out of the horrible pit (Psalm 40:2). And He does so simply in enabling us to receive God's testimony concerning this wondrous Rock, concerning the free love of Him who is our rock and refuge.

Trust ye in the LORD for ever: for in the LORD Jehovah is everlasting strength (Isaiah 26:4); the Rock of Ages.

Day 6

Deliverance for the Sorrowful

Thou wilt save the afflicted people.
– Psalm 18:27

To be numbered among "the afflicted people," need not discourage us. We are not thereby made outcasts, as if God were shaking us off like withered leaves to leave us to perish and think of us no more. He will *save the afflicted people.* This was the confidence that David knew to place in Him when brought very low, and this was the confidence with which a Greater than David leaned upon Him when He was brought lower still.

It is salvation that the afflicted need. Their situation is a much more desperate one than they imagine, however sharp and sad be the stroke that wounds them. It is not mere help or comfort or relief that they need. It is salvation. Their saddest situation needs no more, but their least affliction needs no less.

And in God there is salvation for them. He who afflicts is the same who delivers. The smiter is the

Savior. The wounder is the healer. Into His hands we commend ourselves so that He may take over for us. He who is our God is the God of salvation, and this is enough both to assure us that the trial will not be too bitter and that deliverance will come in due time. When it comes, it will be complete.

There is no real evil in affliction, except that which we put into it ourselves by our perversity. There is only good. Not to be afflicted is the worst affliction that can come upon us.

The Soul's True Sun

In His favor is life.
– Psalm 30:5

I f the sun were to be blotted out of the heavens, every leaf and flower would wither; life would cease. Without sunshine, the earth would be a desert.

Jehovah is the sun of the soul. Without His beams, all is not merely darkness; it is death. His love is the sunlight that gladdens and revives us. Where that love is shed down, all is peace; where that love is withheld, all is sadness and terror and gloom. Life is not life when this love is hidden. In His favor is life. The favor of others may cheer us for an hour and make us forget our weariness, but it leaves the soul as heavy and dark as before. It does not comfort, it does not quicken, it does not heal or refresh. Only of God's love can it be said that in it is life.

Yes, it contains life for us, the true life of the soul, and he who finds this favor, finds life. The possession of that favor is blessedness. And this favor is not hard to find. It does not need to be bought. It is freely given. We just have to take it. Like the sunshine, it is around us, and we only have to let it in. God sends us the good news of it in the gospel of His grace, and he who simply receives that gospel is at once put in possession of the divine favor, the whole free love of God, which is in Christ Jesus our Lord. And so the apostle says, *We have known and believed the love that God hath to us* (1 John 4:16).

Let God Plan for You

~

My times are in Thy hand.
– Psalm 31:15

These are Christ's words, for the psalm is one of His utterances when bearing our sins. He is speaking as the "sent" one, the dependent, trusting Son of man.

We, too, can claim these words. We look up and remember Jehovah. What He is, even apart from what He is to us, is our joy. He is Jehovah; He is the disposer of times and events, the sovereign arranger of everything relating to us. We are creatures, sinners, worms; yet He is so condescendingly mindful of us that He orders our whole life and lot. The God of love holds our times in His hand.

1. What solemnity, then, this casts over life! A life completely ordered in all its times by the infinite Jehovah must be a solemn thing.

2. What stability it imparts! Even in such an unstable world, everything is under the regulation of an unchanging purpose.

3. What certainty it gives to everything that happens! There can be no random, no trivial events; nothing disjointed or loose.

4. What peace it fills us with in this tempestuous age! Empires may rock to and fro, statesmen stagger, confusion reign; we are at peace. All is well.

5. What consolation in sorrow! Our times are in hands, divinely wise and powerful. All must work for good. There can be no real evil.

6. What hope for the future! We know that there is light beyond this gloom. The storm lasts for an hour; the calm that follows is eternal.

Day 9

The True Burden Bearer

Cast thy burden on the Lord,
and he shall sustain thee.
– Psalm 55:22

We do not need to bear our own burdens any more than we need to bear our own sins. God has provided for the bearing of both. He takes them upon Himself. The work of burden bearing is as completely His as is the work of sin bearing. His love has removed all necessity for our attempting to bear either the one or the other.

Even if we could, then, why should we bear them? It is not wise. Instead, it is foolish beyond measure, and it is as useless as it is foolish.

But more than this, it is sinful. To try to be our own sin bearers is to make void the work of Christ as our sin bearer; so to try to be our own burden bearers is to make void His work as our burden bearer. We see the sin of trying to bear our own guilt; let us learn to see as clearly the sin of seeking to bear our own burdens. Let us understand the sin of not casting our burden on the Lord.

What is there about these burdens that we should be so unwilling to part with them? Or what is there about God that should make us unwilling to cast them on Him? His love and power and faithfulness all invite us to do this. Not to do it is to suspect and distrust Him. He delights to bear the whole undivided weight; shall we not, then, give up every burden to Him who wants us to be without concern (1 Corinthians 7:32) because He cares for us! What sweet and holy lightness of spirit would then be ours! The burden is not lessened in itself, but it is borne by the Mighty God!

Day 10

Still Trust

Trust in Him at all times.
– Psalm 62:8

One of God's heaviest complaints against us is that we will not trust Him. There is nothing that He desires so much as this. There is nothing that honors Him so much as this. There is nothing that would bring so many blessings to ourselves; yet we do not trust Him. We speak of Him, but we do not trust Him. We pray to Him, but we do not trust Him.

Have we any good reason for this distrust? Is God's character such as to repel our trust? Has He shown us so much ill will that we dare not trust Him? Surely there are no reasons in Him for distrust! His whole character and actions toward us are such as to draw out our most hearty trust. His love, His grace, His long-suffering – all these revealed and pledged to us in the gift of His beloved Son – show us what a God we have and how entirely worthy of our trust He is.

Nor can anything in us, however evil, be a reason for not trusting Him. Our sins may be many, our hearts may be hard, our wills may be crooked, our ways very rebellious; but all these together are no reason for distrusting God. To distrust Him because of these would be adding sin to sin. He is *rich in mercy* (Ephesians 2:4), He is *the God of all grace* (1 Peter 5:10); let us *trust in Him at all times* (Psalm 62:8). Simple trust in Him as the God of all grace would do for us what nothing else could do. We will not be losers by our confidence.

Day 11

Fulness for the Empty

He satisfieth the longing soul.
– Psalm 107:9

It is our poverty that fits us for the riches of God. This is our only qualification. It is with the poor that God deals. It is the empty that He fills.

We are very unwilling to be thought wholly poor or completely empty. And this is the real hindrance to our being blessed! If we were always willing to be treated as such, we would soon find what blessing would pour in. Then the great barrier would be taken away.

When a soul comes to know that it is really poor and empty, then it stretches out its hands to Him who alone can satisfy. It is in this attitude that God meets us. He satisfies the longing soul. Should we not come before Him in this way? He wants no merit, no claim on our part. All He desires is that we should be willing to be receivers. He asks no more. He loves to bless. He gives to all men liberally, and He does not find fault

(James 1:5). Let us go to Him. He sends no one away empty.

Each longing cry that goes up to His ears meets with a ready response. He is not slow to give. His love is not as our love; His thoughts are not as our thoughts; His ways are not as our ways (Isaiah 55:8). He gave His Son, and what will He not give? He has sent His Spirit, and what will not that Spirit bring to us? He has made known to us His gospel – His good news. How much does that imply? How can we be poor with such riches as His at our side?

Look to Him Who Made You

*Thy hands have made me and fash-
ioned me: give me understanding, that
I may learn thy commandments.*
– Psalm 119:73

I t was in the same way that Peter wrote ages after: *Commit the keeping of their souls to him in well doing, as unto a faithful Creator* (1 Peter 4:19). Both the Old and New Testament saints are looking at God as the God who made them – not merely the God who clothes the lilies and feeds the ravens – but the God who made themselves. On this they build their trust. He made them, and He has not unmade them. Surely, they may trust Him. They seem to say to God, "You have made us: surely You will teach us. Surely You will preserve and comfort us. The God who created us will not forsake the work of His own hands. He who gave us breath, will He not much more give us His Holy

Spirit? He who cares for these vile bodies, will He not much more care for these souls?"

This is a peace-giving truth. It is a strong and blessed argument against all unbelief. We cannot deny that He made us; surely, we cannot doubt that He will care for us and keep us and bless us. It is like Paul's argument in Romans 8:32: *He that spared not his own Son, but delivered him up for us all, how shall he not with him also freely give us all things?* He who upholds us in being and keeps us out of hell, what will He not do for us? What will He not give us? Would He give us our daily life, with all its common mercies, if He were only seeking to destroy us?

Day 13

Water for the Thirsty

～

I will pour water upon him that is thirsty,
and floods upon the dry ground.
– Isaiah 44:3

Most tender are the compassions of our God. Most affectionate is the interest that He takes in our welfare. His thoughts toward us are thoughts of peace. He does not weary in well-doing toward us in spite of all our ill-doing toward Him.

He desires to see us happy, and He gives us His promise that He will make us so. He does so in a way that shows us that nothing will be able to hinder our being happy if we will allow Him to make us so. "Let Me make you happy; let Me fill you with My joy." This is how He speaks to us.

He knows what a thirsty land we dwell in, a desert where there are no springs of water and no shady palm trees. He sees how certain we are to be thirsty in such a world, and He provides for it. *I will pour water upon him that is thirsty*; no, I will pour *floods upon the dry ground.* These souls of ours are like the earth we dwell in – dry ground. But here is the promise of the welcome shower. It comes from God Himself. It is from His free love that the refreshing rain descends; it is that free love that is itself the reviving rain. Let us lay our parched and weary souls under it so that we may be made fresh and glad. These showers, these floods from heaven can refresh the most withered and drooping.

Day 14

Strength for the Helpless

*In the Lord have I righteous-
ness and strength.*
– Isaiah 45:24

These are the two things we needed most – righteousness for our unrighteousness and strength for our helplessness. "I am unrighteous" is our feeling every moment. To meet this, a divine righteousness is at hand. "I am without strength" is our feeling also. But it was because we were without strength that Christ died for us. And, besides, there is strength provided – divine strength, strength as free and perfect and near as is the righteousness. This strength completely meets our complaint of inability. The truth is that we are far more helpless than we think ourselves. Yet that does not matter. It is to them that have no might that He increases strength (Isaiah 40:29). We ought, then, no more to be cast down by a sense of inability than by a sense of unworthiness. God has provided against both. There is enough strength at our disposal not only to make our inability no real hindrance but also to make it the very thing that gives us hope, inasmuch as it draws out the strength that is in the Lord for us. It gives Him an opportunity for magnifying His strength in our weakness. Most gladly, then, let us glory in our infirmities so that the power of Christ may rest upon us (2 Corinthians 12:9). It is in this way that out of weakness we are made strong.

Day 15

A Present Righteousness

⌒

I bring near My righteousness.
– Isaiah 46:13

God is here speaking to those who are *far from righteousness* (Isaiah 46:12), and He proposes to remedy their evil and to remove this distance by bringing His righteousness near to them. They will not come near to His righteousness. They keep aloof from it. In great love, therefore, He resolves to bring it near to them.

And He has brought it near! It is as near as it is possible for anything to be to us, as near as the words themselves which tell us of it. What can be nearer to us than words which not only float round us but which, entering by the ear, go through our whole man? The apostle shows us in the tenth chapter of Romans how near this righteousness is. We do not need to go up to heaven for it nor to go down into the earth for it. We do not need to go one step nor to move one inch in order to reach it. It is so near as to be within the reach of every sinner to whom the good news is preached. We know that it is free, that it is precious, that it is sufficient, that it is suitable; but we also know that it is *near.* If it were far off, it would not do any good for us. But it is so near that we have nothing to do in order to get it, except to consent to let God put it on us! This is faith. Oh, let us not thrust away the Hand that would clothe us with raiment so necessary and so divine!

Day 16

God's Cure for Darkness

Who is among you that feareth the
LORD, that obeyeth the voice of his ser-
vant, that walketh in darkness, and
hath no light? let him trust in the name
of the LORD, and stay upon his God.
– Isaiah 50:10

Our way is often dark in this dark world. Evil and sorrow surround us like thick clouds that shut out the light. What, then, shall we do when we are on the point of losing our way? Take hold of God's hand, as the little child does of its father's in the dark night, and keep close to His side.

This is God's cure for darkness – simple confidence in Himself. The lack of this confidence puts us all wrong. The possession of it keeps us all right.

But am I warranted in trusting God at all times, whatever may be the evil that I feel to be in me? Of course you are, just as you are bound to obey the command which says you should love Him with all your heart (Matthew 22:37). You would not say, "I am so bad that I am not justified in loving God." That would be adding sin to sin. So, you ought never to say, "I am so bad that I am not entitled to trust God." God commands you to trust Him, and not to do so would just be adding sin to sin. Trust Him at all times, for He is worthy to be trusted. Stay upon Him, for His arm is strong enough to bear the whole weight both of yourself and your sins. Do not hesitate or delay. Trust Him at once and as you are. Trust Him now.

Day 17

The Man of Sorrows

~~~~

His visage was so marred
more than any man.
– Isaiah 52:14

He of whom the prophet speaks is the same as is said to be *fairer than the children of men* (Psalm 45:2). Yet, behold, He is so marred that He has *no form nor comeliness* (Isaiah 53:2)! Once fairer than all, now more disfigured than any!

1. Earth's climate did not suit this *tender plant* (Isaiah 53:2). The air was not genial like that of heaven, from where He had come; and the soil had the curse on it. How could it do anything but wither?

2. Inward grief consumed Him. Like a fire within, His sorrow dried up His freshness until He became *like a bottle in the smoke* (Psalm 119:83).

3. Man's hatred struck Him. Each day He met the contradiction of sinners against Himself. He was

forced to say, *Reproach hath broken my heart* (Psalm 69:20), and the reproach that broke His heart could not help but mar His face.

4. God's wrath came down on Him. Often in the days of His flesh, He was constrained to cry, *Thy wrath lieth hard upon me* (Psalm 88:7). This wrath could not fail to mar His visage. Was there ever wrath like this? And was there ever any of the sons of men so likely to be affected by that wrath? His holiness, His heavenliness made Him feel that wrath even more. No wonder that His visage was marred more than any man.

That much-marred face is our light and healing. We look at it and are enlightened. We look at it and are healed, for every line of sadness on it, every wrinkle of grief speaks to us of love.

Day 18

God's Desire to Be Known

—〜—

Ye shall know that I am the Lord.
– Ezekiel 7:4

I t is God's desire that He should be known. Even more, it is His purpose that He should be known. He will compel even His enemies to know Him. If they will not know Him in His love, they will know Him in His wrath. If they will not know Him in His pardons, they will know Him in His judgments.

It is, however, a blessed thought for us that God wishes to be known. There is no hiding Himself, no retiring out of view. He is not unwilling to show Himself. In fact, His object in all that He says and does is to so reveal Himself that it will be impossible for anyone not to know Him. Considering what God has done to unfold His glorious character, we are led to wonder why He should still be to so many *the unknown God* (Acts 17:23).

It is life to know Him (John 17:3). It is peace to be acquainted with Him (Job 22:21). And if He is so willing to be known, why should any of us remain ignorant of Him? Should we not go straight to Him so that He may teach us to know Himself? If He is so desirous that even those who are turning away from Him should know Him, will He hide His love or veil His glory from those who are seeking His face?

The knowledge of Jehovah! What is there of peace and light and joy that is not contained in that!

Day 19

Be Quite Sure of Getting

Ask, and it shall be given you.
– Matthew 7:7

We sometimes feel our need of certain things but are sad because we think them beyond our reach. If they were within sight or within touch, like the grass under our feet or like the river that flows by our house, we would feel certain of getting them; but they seem to us far off, and we lose all hope of ever having them.

This is unbelief. It is dealing with God as if He were not the God of all grace. It is using prayer as if it were not the means of obtaining what we need, and it is treating His promises as if they were not meant to be kept.

Now, we ought never to ask if the thing that we desire is out of sight or far off or difficult or costly but simply, has God commanded us to come to Him for it? Whatever we are entitled to ask for is as truly within our reach as is the flower at our side, which we have only to stoop down and pluck. Therefore, God has placed every spiritual blessing within our reach because He has told us to pray for them. Is it His own Holy Spirit that we desire, is it more faith, a truer sense of sin, warmer love, or a holier life? Let us never feel as if any of these things were far off or hard to be gotten. They are at hand. They wait only for us to ask. They are within God's reach, and therefore, they are within ours because they are the things that He has taught us to ask for.

Day 20

The Servant of Sinners

~

I am among you as he that serveth.
– Luke 22:27

In the kingdom of Christ, the lowest place is the place of honor. It was this that He Himself stooped to when He took upon Him the form of a servant.

It was in lowly love that He came to serve us, and what is there that He is not willing to stoop to in order that He may supply our need? He has already stooped to the cradle, the cross, and the tomb, and what is there, after these, that He will shrink from or refuse in the way of service for us?

He has taken on Him this special office; will He not perform it well? What need is there, be it great or small, that He will not supply? In going to Him for this supply, we are not taxing His patience, we are not making undue demands upon Him, we are not making too free with His love or condescension. We are only employing Him in the very way in which He delights to be employed. We are only making that use of His condescension that the Father designed when He filled Him with the Spirit without measure and sent Him to us so that He might *supply all your need according to His riches in glory* (Philippians 4:19). We cannot be too needy or too empty. We cannot apply to Him too often or too urgently. He is as unwearied in His service as in His love.

Day 21

Peace in Christ

—~—

These things I have spoken unto you,
that in me ye might have peace.
– John 16:33

There is peace for us; yes, *peace*, even in a world of evil and unrest. Whatever shadows may fling themselves across our path or rest above our homes, there is peace. We do not need to be troubled or sad.

It is not man that speaks it. It is the Son of God. He makes known the gladdening truth. He says, "There is peace," and He tells us where it is to be found – in Himself. *He is our peace* (Ephesians 2:14), and the peace *which passeth all understanding* (Philippians 4:7) is in Him alone. In me you shall have peace (John 16:33). *Peace I leave with you, my peace I give unto you* (John 14:27).

Yet again, He tells us that it is through what He has spoken to us that we are to get this peace that is in Him. His words are the words of peace. They lead us to Himself. They make known the grace that is in

Him. They tell us what He is as well as what He has done. To listen to the words that Christ has spoken is to drink in the peace of which He is the fountain. In hearing Him, peace flows in upon us like a river. It is only by closing our ear against Him and against His words that we can shut out the blessed peace.

How little do people know how much they lose in not listening to His voice and how much they would gain by listening!

The Sinner's Substitute

Christ died for our sins.
– 1 Corinthians 15:3

If Christ, then, has died, why should we die? It was once necessary that every sinner should die for his sins, but it no longer is. If the sinner now dies, it is because he is resolved to do so; because he will have nothing to do with the Substitute. That Substitute is the Son of God, who suffered for sin – the just for the unjust. He is not far off but at hand. He is a sufficient, a willing, a loving Substitute.

It is not our money nor our merits that He asks; it is simply our consent. He was willing to become the sin bearer; are we willing that He should become our sin bearer? The Father consents, the Son consents, the Holy Spirit consents; do we consent? Then the great transaction is done; the great exchange is made. He gets our sins; we get His righteousness. He gets our death;

we get His life. For what is faith but our consenting to have Him for our Security and Substitute?

Here we rest. We hand over to Him all our sins and burdens. He takes them from us and buries them out of sight in His own grave. No one, except the Divine Substitute, can relieve us of our guilt. No one else can remove our fears or give rest to our troubled conscience. He can and will do it all. For this He died and rose again. For this He ascended on high and ever lives to intercede (Hebrews 7:25).

Day 23

Christ Our Peace

~~~~

He is our peace.
– Ephesians 2:14

It was peace that we needed; for sin had thrown us out of peace by troubling the conscience and coming in between us and God. It was peace that we needed; for without peace, what is life?

It is peace that Christ has made. He has not left it for us to make. He has made it on the cross, leaving nothing that is necessary for our peace undone. Faith simply apprehends what Christ has made. Unbelief tries to make peace, but faith takes it as already made and rejoices in it. All that hindered our having peace has been taken away, and all that could cause trouble of conscience has been fully met by the work of the Great Substitute on the cross.

The cross is the display of righteous love, love coming to us from God in a righteous way. We lift up our eyes to the cross and see the Son of God there bearing sin.

Then the love flows into us. The more that we allow the thoughts of this free love to find their way into us, the deeper and more abiding will be our peace. We are like people placed in an atmosphere filled with fragrance and health. We only have to inhale it. The gospel has surrounded us with this atmosphere of free love. Let us open our mouths and breathe this blessed air. It will at once revive and refresh us. We will find what health and vigor it can impart!

Day 24

The Threefold Blessing

*Peace be to the brethren, and love
with faith, from God the Father
and the Lord Jesus Christ.*
– Ephesians 6:23

Peace, love, faith; these are the three things that the apostle desired for the brethren, remembering, no doubt, what had come to himself – *the grace of our Lord was exceeding abundant with faith and love which is in Christ Jesus* (1 Timothy 1:14). This threefold blessing comes directly from the Father and the Son, through the Holy Spirit sent down from heaven.

"I need peace." Yes, and it is this that the Father gives. It is this that Jesus gives. Both Father and Son desire that you should have it. Allow them to give it.

"I need love." Yes, and it is this which the Father and the Son bestow. They hold it out to you. They will not only teach you their own vast love but also to love in return.

"I need faith." Yes, surely you do. And the whole Godhead presents it to you. *It is the gift of God* (Ephesians 2:8). Lord, increase our faith! Lord, help our unbelief!

Go, then, trustingly to God, to the Father and the Son so that you may get at once the peace, love, and faith that you need so much. Confide in the free love of Godhead. You will find in this simple confidence the cure for all spiritual diseases, the channel of all health and blessing. Distrust will do nothing for you. It will only make you worse. Unreserved confidence will do everything for you. God asks this. Give Him His request.

Day 25

Give God Your Cares to Keep

～

Be careful for nothing; but in every thing by
prayer and supplication with thanksgiving
let your requests be made known unto God.
– Philippians 4:6

We do not need to bear our own sins, for Christ has borne them on the cross. Nor do we need to bear our own cares, for He is the bearer of our cares as well as of our sins. *He hath borne our griefs, and carried our sorrows* (Isaiah 53:4). *If any man sin, we have an advocate with the Father, Jesus Christ the righteous* (1 John 2:1) so we have only to take our sins to Him so that they may be forgiven. *If we confess our sins, he is faithful and just to forgive us our sins* (1 John 1:9). In the same way, let us go to Him with our cares. He is as willing to take them from us as our sins. Let us not keep them to ourselves nor try to bear them with our own strength.

Why should we insist on bearing our own cares

when He is so ready to bear them for us? Why do we magnify them and multiply them and brood over them, as if in so doing we could relieve ourselves or make them seem fewer and lighter? Let us go with them at once to Him, knowing that it is as self-righteous to keep our cares as our sins from Him. Let us go to Him with thanksgiving as well as prayer (Philippians 4:6). Oh, how thanksgiving lightens all burdens and scatters all shadows! How quickly care leaves us when we rebuke it with, *Bless the Lord, O my soul* (Psalm 103:1).

Day 26

Divine Fulness

~~~

It pleased the Father that in Him
should all fulness dwell.
– Colossians 1:19

There is no fulness like this. It is fulness provided by the Father Himself. It is the infinite fulness of the eternal Son, the God-man. It is all fulness. It is fulness of the very kind that sinners need. It is fulness for us. There is fulness of pardon, fulness of life, fulness of grace, fulness of righteousness, fulness of strength, fulness of wisdom. For *Jesus Christ, who of God is made unto us wisdom, and righteousness, and sanctification, and redemption* (1 Corinthians 1:30).

Is there, then, any reason for our remaining empty? That fulness is at our side and ready to flow into us. How unreasonable, then, are our desponding complaints of emptiness and leanness! What can despondency mean when God has provided such a fulness of every blessing?

And in what light does God view such despondency but as our refusal to be blessed?

It is of this fulness that the Holy Spirit takes and pours into us. It is His part first to make us willing to receive it and then to pour it in. How willing is the whole Godhead – Father, Son, and Spirit – that we should be made partakers of this fulness! *Open thy mouth wide, and I will fill it* (Psalm 81:10).

We need not, then, be poor, as long as Christ is rich; nor need we be weak as long as He is strong. God's desire is that we should partake of this fulness, and His delight is in seeing us filled.

Day 27

Everlasting Consolation

~~~

*Our Lord Jesus Christ himself, and God,
even our Father, which hath loved us,
and hath given us everlasting consolation and good hope through grace.*
– 2 Thessalonians 2:16

It is both of the Father and of the Son that the apostle speaks. The love of Godhead is what he presents to us. He loved us, and so, the name we get is, *Beloved of God* (Romans 1:7). He loved us and gave His Son for us. He loved us and gave us eternal life in Him. He loved us and gave us *everlasting consolation and good hope.*

God's free love is the great fountainhead of our consolation. The very thought of it is comfort, but the rich supplies of comfort that it administers are far beyond that which comes from merely remembering the love. God pours in the consolation. In spite of sorrow, He comforts. No earthly grief is able to resist the power of consolation so almighty, so divine. It forces back the tide of sorrow, and in its place, brings not merely submission but also gladness.

Everlasting consolation! This is what we are given. *Good hope* – hope of His coming and of the long-promised glory; *hope through grace* – through that free love which first picked us up when lying in our sins. This is the hope that endures! What sorrow here can withstand the comfort that comes from a hope so full of blessedness and glory? With this consolation and this hope, let us go on our way in peace. What or who can dishearten or dismay us?

The Lord's Tender Love

The Lord is very piti-
ful, and of tender mercy.
– James 5:11

This suits us well. It takes in all that we need. We need pity, for we are often sad and weary, and here is the pity that we need. Our God is pitiful, yes, very pitiful. His pity, like Himself, is truly infinite. It knows no bounds. It is not narrow nor feeble nor changeable. It is wide as the bosom out of which came the Eternal Son, the *unspeakable gift* (2 Corinthians 9:15). Nothing in us can alter it, lessen it, or make it flow less freely. It is a father's pity, which no unworthiness nor unthankfulness can change or check. A child's unhappiness, from whatever cause, stirs the father's pity; so, our wants, weaknesses, cares, fears, and sorrows call up new pity in the bosom of Him who is very pitiful. Whether we will believe it or not, He pities us; and He pities us all the more when He sees the unhappiness to which our unbelief exposes us.

There is also mercy for us, for we are always sinning, rebelling, murmuring, going astray. It is abundant mercy. It is *tender mercy*, or, as we read elsewhere, *tender mercies, a multitude of thy tender mercies* (Psalm 69:16). This is enough, even for the most sinful. The thought of these tender mercies keeps the soul in peace, even when all things in us and about us speak of trouble and war.

Day 29

Keep the Joy in View

Who for the joy that was set before
Him endured the cross.
– Hebrews 12:2

Christ's cross was the heaviest ever borne, yet He bore it. Its pains were the sharpest that ever tore the frame of man, yet He endured them. No cross of ours can ever be like His, yet He endured it. He went up to it without a murmur.

What made Him so willing to endure the cross, so patient under its shame and agony? It was the joy set before Him. He looked forward to the joy that lay beyond the cross, and He bore it gladly. It was that joy that made it so easy to bear.

Our cross is sometimes hard to bear. Grief comes on grief until we are quite bowed down. Burden presses on burden until we are ready to faint. The way is long and rough and dark. We get weary and troubled.

In such a time, what is our relief? The joy set before

us. This lifts us up. This smoothes our brow. This dries our tears. This nerves us with new strength. The joy set before us! How cheering is the hope! For it is unspeakable and everlasting. And it will be here so soon! What is one hour's darkness to the eternal sunshine? What is one night's tossing on the roaring deep to the calm of the everlasting haven? What are the tears of the night to the joy of the bright morning and the triumphant jubilee of the unending day? *Weeping may endure for a night, but joy cometh in the morning* (Psalm 30:5).

Day 30

Remember Your Creator

Thou hast created all things.
– Revelation 4:11

He who made things to exist must be the I Am. The Creator's name is Yahweh. And this is the God we relate to. The Maker of heaven and earth is our God.

The word creation is familiar to us. We think we understand it. In truth we do not. The idea is an unfathomable one. It is one of the deepest things of God. Who knows what it is to create except He who creates? Things that were not, are, when He speaks. This is all we know.

Here is the link between the seen and the unseen, the connection between the outer and the inner circle of being. Here is the tie between this universe of ours and God. It is a tie closer, firmer, and more abiding than any other. In comparison with it, all the ties we are accustomed to speak of as tender or endearing are as a thread or straw. Yet who among us feels either the strength or the blessedness of this peculiar tie? Was it not to this that Job appealed when he said, *Is it good unto thee that Thou shouldest oppress, that thou shouldest despise the work of thine hands?* (Job 10:3). Might we not use it too, and say, "O Lord, You have made, will You not bless me?"

The God who made these starry heavens and this green earth is the God whose love is all to us and in loving whom is the very joy of joys. His love in the new creation is no doubt the highest of all, but let us not forget His love in the old creation to which David and Job appealed.

Day 31

The Eternal Well

~~~

I will give unto him that is athirst of the
fountain of the water of life freely.
– Revelation 21:6

It is as if Christ had said, "Is there any one on earth who wants to be happy but does not know how? Let him come to Me, and I will give him all that he needs."

Christ spoke these words from heaven, showing us that His love is the same in heaven as it was on earth. He spoke them especially for those who should live in the last days, for they come in at the close of the book, just after it had been said, *It is done* (Revelation 21:6). We ought to feel as if the message was especially meant for us who are living so far down the ages and so near the day of His coming.

Just when He is about to come, He looks down on a miserable world, as He did on Jerusalem, and sends before Him this declaration of His love. How unwilling is He to smite, how willing to save. How desirous is He that we should drink the living water and be made partakers of the joy that there is in Himself for us! *Whosoever will, let him take the water of life freely* (Revelation 22:17).

Behold, I come quickly (Revelation 22:12). *Behold, I come as a thief* (Revelation 16:15). He warns us, yet side by side with the warning He sets the invitation, *I will give unto him that is athirst of the fountain of the water of life freely.*

Do You Know Your Maker?

None saith, Where is God my maker,
who giveth songs in the night.
– Job 35:10

H e who made all things to be must be the *I Am*. Who but Yahweh, the Being of beings, can create? Who but *the Beginning and the Ending* (Revelation 1:8) could create in the beginning? All within the circle of the universe, upper and under, is of His creating. He must be above and beyond that circle; greater, brighter, and more glorious than all that it contains.

This is the God to whom we belong. He made us for Himself, and He made that universe for us. The Creator of heaven and earth is our God. Have I learned in loving peacefulness of spirit to say, "He is mine"? His making me for Himself shows that He desires my fellowship. His making this fair world for me shows that He seeks my happiness. Is He not then one I can confide in and commune with? Has He done anything to estrange Himself from me or repel my confidence? Has He not done everything to draw me to Himself and win my unwilling love?

I dwell beneath the blue of His bright heaven; I walk upon the face of His fair earth. Shall I not lean on Him? Shall I not love Him? Shall I not lay myself to rest each night upon His breast as the child upon the bosom of its mother? Is it not in this way that I am to commit my soul *to him in well doing, as unto a faithful Creator* (1 Peter 4:19)?

Day 33

Delight Yourself in God

～

O taste and see that the Lord is good:
blessed is the man that trusteth in him.
– Psalm 34:8

To delight myself in God must be the very life of my life, the very sunshine of my days. I am made for this, and nothing else can satisfy.

All the gifts of God – the sun, the sky, the stars, the flowers, the streams – are intended to facilitate this delighting in God, to be instruments for carrying it on and intensifying it.

Should I then take these gifts and use them for the purpose of making myself happy without God? If the thoughts of God are pleasant to my spirit, then these gifts will be used for augmenting, developing, and perpetuating such thoughts. If I have no joy in thinking of God, then these gifts will assuredly be perverted to the awful purpose of excluding God, drowning the thoughts of God, of making me happy without the necessity of having recourse to God at all!

Is not this what thousands are deliberately doing? Is not the whole system of their life based upon the principle of being happy, easy, and comfortable without God? Is it not their object to draw so largely upon the gifts as to enable them to live without thinking of the Giver at all? *My soul, come not thou into their secret* (Genesis 49:6).

This preference of created things to God may do for a few years, but what will eternity be to those who have no God to delight in?

When Will You Turn?

To day if ye will hear his voice,
harden not your heart.
– Psalm 95:7-8

Your time on earth, O man, is only a day! These limbs will soon cease to move, these eyes will close, that heart will no longer throb, and all that you call life will soon be done!

Is it not then time to turn? Have you calculated the chances and weighed the opportunities of your coming years so that you can quietly sit down and say, "I will wait. I intend to turn, but not now." Yet God urges you with His *now*. Your word is tomorrow, but His word is *today*. Will you not then turn now? You must turn some time or other or else be lost. Why not *now*? Can you afford to trifle with your last breath? Is it of so little value in your eyes? Ah, time, time! It may seem nothing now, but it will soon be all, and you will learn its preciousness when all is over.

Can you afford to trifle with your souls? Have they so little value in your eyes that you can sport them away or sell them for a few vain pleasures? Ah, that soul! The seat of such joy and grief, that soul, will you allow it to be destroyed?

Can you afford to trifle with sin? Is it nothing to you? Is that which God hates so infinitely a mere word or sound?

Can you afford to trifle with God? And will He be trifled with? *Be not deceived; God is not mocked* (Galatians 6:7).

Can you afford to trifle with Christ and His blood? Is the Savior nothing? Is His blood a common thing? Oh, awake from your miserable sleep. Awake and turn! It must be *now*!

Day 35

Are You Ready?

~

*There shall in no wise enter into
it any thing that defileth.*
– Revelation 21:27

There is a life to come and a world to come! Our course on earth will be ended soon. The place that knew us will know us no more. We will have passed away out of all that grieves or gladdens us here.

What, then, are your hopes? What is that eternity to be that will so soon receive you? Whatever it may be, it can be no unimportant thing to you. A whole eternity of being! That, surely, may startle and arouse you. What you are or have here on earth concerns you very little, for what is your life? It is a vapor. But what you are to be and to have hereafter concerns you much. This life is but a dream; the life to come is real.

Are you, then, ready to pass on into that eternity? Are all preparations made and your well-being secured so that you can enter it without a fear? Or has no preparation been made? Is there nothing but darkness overhanging you, so that you shrink from the sick bed and the death bed and the tomb?

Have you been born from above? Born of the Spirit, born the second time, born of God? These are the marks of a soul prepared to pass into the eternal mansions. Are these marks traceable on you? Have you been made partaker of this better birth, this birth which, while it marks the sonship, secures the heirship and the kingdom?

Day 36

The Evil of Sin

——~——

The soul that sinneth, it shall die.
– Ezekiel 18:4

One sin casts the angels out of heaven. One sin blights paradise and ruins a race. One sin spreads itself out, not over a region, but over a world. One sin propagates itself and overflows, not one generation, but generations for thousands of years. One sin contains enough in its one drop to destroy millions upon millions, to destroy them for eternity. What then must sin be! What must be its virulence, its contagiousness, its immeasurable fruitfulness in evil! What havoc it makes among immortal beings! With what a terrific power it is armed!

One sin! Who can count up its consequences? Yet in each of us there are myriads – not one, but myriads of these roots or seeds of evil!

Surely if we realized the woe, the curse that is wrapped up in each of these, we would tremble and be appalled. Our hearts would fail us at the thought. We are poison trees, from whose branches there hang myriads of seeds, seeds that every moment are dropping from us and springing up around.

Yet the divine sin bearer is at hand, ready to deliver, able to undo the evil. Should we not seek His aid? Is not that aid available for us to the full so that life, instead of death, may be ours? *The wages of sin is death; but the gift of God is eternal life through Jesus Christ our Lord* (Romans 6:23).

Day 37

Forsaking the Lord

~~~

Know therefore and see that it is
an evil thing and bitter, that thou
hast forsaken the LORD thy God.
– Jeremiah 2:19

There is not one evil under which we ever groaned that may not be traced to our forsaking the Lord. This is the one root of bitterness that has shot up into a tree of ten thousand branches. There may be other external causes of the evil, but this is the main one. This is the only one that God will recognize as a real cause. As to all the rest, He says, They could have had no power to harm one hair of your head had you not forsaken Me. In keeping close to Me, in leaning on my arm, in abiding under the shadow of my wings, you were absolutely and entirely safe. But in departing from Me, you have exposed yourselves to every form of evil and danger.

These, then, are the lessons our God wants to teach us:

1. We have no one to blame for all the evils that have ever come upon us or our nation or our world but ourselves. We have done it with our own hands.

2. These evils have all flowed from our forsaking God. To be near Him is joy and life; to be far off is woe and death.

3. The true cure for them is our returning to Him whom we have forsaken. No other cure will be effectual. They will not reach the real seat and cause of the disease.

Long-wandering sinner, will you not return and be blessed? Why should you die in the far country when there is bread enough to spare in your Father's house?

Man, His Own Destroyer

~~~

Hast thou not procured this unto thyself?
– Jeremiah 2:17

The power of the creature to do evil is as striking as is his powerlessness to undo it. He has power to blight a world, though he has no power to restore freshness to one faded leaf. He can kill, but he cannot make alive again one worm beneath his feet. He can ruin to an infinite extent; he cannot rectify one displaced atom.

What terrible responsibility is this? The thought of it is able to act on us with power.

1. It startles. Am I, a creature, a sinner, really possessed of such power of evil? How then can I be careless as to the very least thing I do?

2. It saddens. Oh, what sorrow is likely to be mine – doing all manner of evil yet undoing none! Blighting everything but freshening nothing!

3. It overawes. What an infinite greatness this confers on me! What stupendous importance it attaches to everything in life! Every word or action tells either for evil or good; there is nothing little, nothing unmeaning.

4. It solemnizes. In such a case, there is no room for levity. Life becomes a solemn thing. Keep far away all frivolity, indulgence, and idleness!

5. It animates. If this is my responsibility, then I have no time to lose. Get up and start doing! Lay out every moment well. For I can recall nothing; I can undo nothing. For good or for evil, there it stands.

Day 39

The Sinner Returning

—〜—

When he came to himself, he said,
How many hired servants of my
father's have bread enough and to
spare, and I perish with hunger! I
will arise and go to my father.
– Luke 15:17-18

When he "comes to himself," he begins to think of the happy home he had left. He calls to mind his father and his father's house. He sees famine all around. No kindness meets him or delivers him from poverty. Then he remembers the home of his youth.

When the sinner comes to himself, he begins to think of God. He had been trying to be happy without God, but it will not do. All refuge fails him. He is thoroughly miserable. The world is unkind and empty. Its fountains have run dry. He calls to mind his forsaken God and thinks on the love that he might have been enjoying. To Him he must return. If there is refuge for him anywhere, it must be with Him. If his needs are to be supplied and his sorrows soothed, it must be by the hand of this Father. For a father is a father still, whatever may be the wickedness of a wayward son. He has heard of the free love of God shown forth in the gift of His Son. He has heard how others, just like him, have been received, and why not he? *I will arise and go.*

And will he succeed? Will he be received? Oh, instead, ask if it is possible that he can be sent away empty? Is it possible that the love that gave the Son can do anything except forgive and bless him?

Day 40

Will You Be Made Whole?

They that be whole need not a phy-
sician, but they that are sick.
– Matthew 9:12

I s it our health that we bring to the physician? No,
not our health, but our sickness. As long as we are
healthy, we do not need him. We only need him when
we are sick.

Yet how many reverse this in spiritual things! The
amount of disease about them seems to discourage
and disqualify. And they labor to find or to make up
some symptoms of returning health in order to qualify
them for the Physician.

They say, " I have no convictions of sin; how can
I come?" Why, if you have no convictions, you have
all the more reason to come, for that proves that you
have more disease about you. They say, "I have no love;
how can I come? Certainly, I am disqualified." Why,
if you have no love, you have more need to come and

are more qualified for the Physician by being more sick. Each disease is a claim on the Physician's skill and power, an appeal to the Physician's tenderness and care. Doubting, troubled spirit, hear this and be encouraged. Be confident and glad. The evils of which you complain are evils that no one but the Savior can remove. Can you, then, bring them too soon? Can you bring too many of them? Are they beyond His power to relieve? And is this your reason for keeping them to yourself and trying to get rid of them before you come? Oh, the folly, as well as the wickedness of unbelief!

The Living Water

~

Ho, every one that thirst-
eth, come ye to the waters.
– Isaiah 55:1

The fountain of these living waters is God Himself. With Him there is the fulness of everything that can refresh, gladden, and bless. There can be no more question, then, that there are such waters than there can be that God is.

If so, then, unhappy soul, you may be happy yet. There is enough in that fountain even for a soul like yours. Your sorrows are not too deep, your troubles are not too many, your thirst is not too great. A fountain such as this is sufficient for them all.

That fountain is sending out its reviving streams. They are flowing through the plains of this parched earth. They are flowing by your side! And they are *free*. "I will give to him who is thirsty of the fountain of the water of life freely" (Revelation 22:17). You must not try to buy them: they are not to be bought by you. And you do not need to, for they are *without money and without price* (Isaiah 55:1).

Are you not thirsty? Are you not saying, "Who will show me any good?" Are you not asking to be made happy yet not knowing how? Then drink abundantly of this fresh well-spring. God invites you to come and quench your thirst. The unhappiness that wearies and oppresses you is just the thirst of which God here speaks, and His saying, "Come to the waters," is just saying, "Come and drink of this river of My free love and be made glad forever."

Day 42

Christ's Welcome

~

Him that cometh to me I will
in no wise cast out.
– John 6:37

Our right to come is full and clear. It is irrespective of anything in us. It presupposes need and sin; nothing more.

The invitation is wide and free. It takes us just as we are, annexing no restriction and demanding no prerequisite. It does not fence itself around with conditions, as if fearful too many might avail themselves of it or as if desirous to keep off the unqualified and the unworthy. It makes no exceptions as to previous life or present character; it welcomes the unworthiest. It forbids none. It leaves no room for suspicion on the part of any. "Come, and come at once; come, and come boldly" is its message to all; for, *him that cometh to me I will in no wise cast out.*

The Promiser is as His promise evidences. His words

and His heart are in harmony. So the free love of the Inviter makes the invitation doubly sure. It is this free love that beckons and begs. It does not stand upon ceremony or insist upon terms. It does not say, "Whosoever comes in this manner or that manner, according to this rule or that rule. But it says, "Whosoever comes I will not cast out." Weary sinner, come at once and be blessed! You do not need to wait as if the Lord Jesus was not quite willing. Hurry and claim the promise. He will show you His love.

Day 43

The Everlasting Gospel

*I saw another angel fly in the midst of
heaven, having the everlasting gospel to
preach unto them that dwell on the earth.*
– Revelation 14:6

It is eternal redemption that is provided for us by the
God-man Redeemer (Hebrews 9:12). So, the gospel,
or good news, concerning this is called "everlasting."
And to this, the apostle Peter refers when contrasting
the withering grass with the enduring word. He says,
*But the word of the Lord endureth for ever. And this
is the word which, by the gospel is preached unto you*
(1 Peter 1:25).

It is not the gospel of one age but the gospel of every
age – everlasting. It is not the gospel of the past age nor
of the present age nor of the age to come but the gospel
of all ages – everlasting.

It is not a gospel whose good news ebbs and flows,
darkens and brightens alternately. It stays the same – for

it is good news of the grace of Him with whom there is no variableness, who is the same yesterday, today, and forever. Our changes cannot affect the gospel, just as they cannot affect Him or make Him less loving, less gracious, less forgiving.

It is a gospel that will carry us through the gloom and weariness of our pilgrimage, even to the end. It is a gospel that will abide with us through eternity, for it is the *everlasting gospel*, and all its blessings are, like itself, everlasting. Everlasting life is the sure inheritance of the believing sinner.

Day 44

The Tender Mercies of God

The LORD is good to all; and his tender mercies are over all his works.
– Psalm 145:9

W hat God does and what God feels must ever be in harmony. If He does what is kind and gracious, it is because He feels so. If He feeds me and clothes me and surrounds me with blessings, it must be because His interest in my welfare is sincere and deep. To suppose otherwise would be to say that while He is speaking and acting in one way, He is in reality feeling in a way totally the opposite.

This cannot be, for all is sincerity with Him. He is not like man, covering over a heart of coldness with the words or acts of love. He feels just as He acts.

That is why I can find the gospel everywhere. To be kept one moment out of hell is of itself marvelous grace. But to be placed, even though a sinner, in a world so fair and sunny, so full of comforts and blessings, is grace more marvelous still. Each rising sun brings me glad tidings of the free love of God. Each bud, each leaf, each flower, each raindrop, preaches to every eye that looks on them glad tidings of the abundant grace of God. For if there is no grace for me, why am I kept here? Why am I surrounded by so many messengers of grace that, day after day, throughout the seasons, meet my ear and eye?

The Love of God

—∼—

Herein is love, not that we loved God,
but that he loved us, and sent his Son
to be the propitiation for our sins.
– 1 John 4:10

How am I to measure the love of God? By the distance between *the throne of the Majesty in the heavens* (Hebrews 8:1) and the grave in which the Son of God was laid. It was an infinite descent, and it is the measure of an infinite love.

How am I to estimate the love of God? By the gift which is so freely sent down to us – the infinite, unspeakable gift. Nothing can equal that gift in value, and nothing can equal that love in greatness.

How am I to understand the love of God? It cannot be understood; it surpasses knowledge. It is beyond the stretch of our thought.

How am I to deserve this love of God? Deserve

it! It is love to the undeserving. This is its essence, its characteristic. It is absolutely free.

How am I to obtain this love of God? By receiving Him who is the embodiment, the incarnation of it. In giving credit to the divine record concerning Him, I let this holy love of God pour itself into my soul, as light streams in upon the body the moment I open my eye to the sun. I look and live. I look and am healed. I look and am blessed forever.

How am I to keep this love of God? By holding the beginning of my confidence steadfast unto the end (Hebrews 3:14). I am to keep hold of it, just as I first took hold of it.

Day 46

Immediate Forgiveness

—～～—

Be of good cheer; thy sins be forgiven thee.
– Matthew 9:2

Many who speak often of forgiveness like to place it beyond their reach so that they may not obtain immediate and certain possession of it, for that would interfere with their self-righteous efforts to work or to pray themselves into the favor of God.

If I am forgiven simply in believing the record that God has given of His Son, then all such efforts are at once superseded and set aside. I will still work, but it will be the working of grateful, happy love. I will still pray, but my praying will be the childlike breathings of the spirit of adoption, the opening of my enlarged heart to a reconciled God.

To place forgiveness beyond the sinner's reach, to place it at the very end of his course, to make it a thing of perpetual doubt is to afford room and excuse for self-righteousness – that very room and excuse that

God, by sending us so free a gospel, has been at such pains to take away. If there is room left for doubting, there will also be room for boasting, whereas God, in making known His free love, meant to leave no room for either.

Come, then, and be forgiven! God is holding out to you the riches of His forgiving love. Why should you hesitate or delay? His desire is to bless you now. Why should you decline an immediate blessing?

The Prevailing Name

~~

*There is none other name under
heaven given among men,
whereby we must be saved.*
– Acts 4:12

In coming to God, I must either use my own name as my plea or another's. In either case, I will be dealt with by God precisely according to the value of the plea; that is, the influence of the name in which I come.

Seeing, then, I am a sinner, to use my own name, either in whole or in part, must lead to my rejection. To use another's will avail me in so far as that other's is acceptable to God, and in so far as God may be willing to let me have the use of that other's name.

Now, there is a name infinitely acceptable to God, a name which He is altogether willing that we should make use of in coming to Him – the name of His own Son.

But the difficulty is to get us to consent to forego the use of our own name and to employ this other.

This is one of the hardest things in the world, yet it is on this that our eternity hinges. As long as I persist in standing before God in my own name, I am a rejected man. The moment I consent to make use of the name of Christ, that moment I am accepted and I am dealt with according to the value and worth of the name on which I have now taken my stand in all my dealings with God. And this is peace! It is such a peace that no amount of conscious unworthiness in me can ever disturb; for it is peace springing from another's merit and coming to me through another's name.

The Sinner's Plea

In thy name shall they rejoice all the day.
– Psalm 89:16

It is this name – the name of Him who is full of grace and truth – that is the beginning as well as the ending of a sinner's confidence and joy. To go to God with this one name as my plea is all I need to secure a large and loving answer.

Why, then, am I hesitating? Why so many doubts? How is there so little confidence in this heart of mine when I bow the knee before the God and Father of our Lord Jesus Christ? It is because I falter in pronouncing the name He loves so well and delights to honor so much. If I doubt or distrust, it must be because I have not fully understood the infinite value of the name and God's willingness to give effect to that name in the case of every sinner who will consent to employ it as a substitute for his own. So that as soon as I learn the value of this name and consent to exchange it for my own, I become *accepted in the beloved* (Ephesians 1:6) and cannot help but rejoice in that name. My joy comes from what I have found in that name. I have found in it a substitute for my own. I have found in it a well of holy love. And because of these things I *rejoice all the day.* When I begin to exchange that name for my own again, immediately, doubting and anxiety ensue. But as long as I set aside my own and employ that name alone, my joy abounds, and my feet stand immovably on the rock that no storm can shake.

True Peace

*The word which God sent unto the children
of Israel, preaching peace by Jesus Christ.*
– Acts 10:36

In order to have peace in my spirit, I must either forget God, falsify His character, or be reconciled to Him through the blood of the cross.

The first of these ways can never be fully carried out, for nothing can ever wholly banish from my thoughts the remembrance of the God who made me. The second of these ways will only lead me down to hell with a lie in my right hand by making me believe that God is indifferent to sin. The third is the only way of permanent, perfect peace.

In being brought near to God, I have peace, for what marred it was my distance from Him. In being reconciled (righteously reconciled), I have peace, for what kept me from having it was the variance between Him and me. This distance has been removed, and this variance adjusted by the sin-bearing work of His Son. Over that work, the great controversy has been settled forever, and a friendship never to be broken has begun between us. This friendship is the very life of my life, the health of my countenance, the joy of my joys.

With God for my friend, I pass through life in peace. He is all to me, and in fellowship with Him, I find a joy that overshadows all that the world calls by that name. With God for my friend, neither weakness, the grave, nor the judgment can alarm my soul. All is well!

Day 50

Will Thinking Well of
Myself Save Me?

—~—

*The Pharisee stood and prayed thus
with himself, God, I thank thee,
that I am not as other men are.*
– Luke 18:11

If in dealing with God, I do or say anything for the
purpose of having a better opinion of myself or of
inducing God to form a better opinion of me and to
deal with me on a better footing than that of a mere
sinner, I am a Pharisee whether I go to the corners of
the streets or not.

Yet how often have I prayed and confessed sin from
this very motive or at least with this object in view! I
have prayed myself into good terms with my own conscience, and when I have confessed sin, I have thought
that surely God must now have a more favorable opinion
of me and deal more gently with me!

Is this all that the gospel has taught me? Have I not learned from it that there can be but one opinion of my case and character? It is that I am a total sinner. And has it not taught me that the very worst opinion I can form of myself cannot be too bad, yet the worst opinion that God can have of me will be no hindrance to His grace or my welcome, provided I am content to take the sinner's place and receive the sinner's welcome? This is the very essence and meaning of the gospel. What more can I desire? What more could God hold out to me? And if all this is not enough to give me confidence, then nothing else will do it, and Christ has died in vain.

Confidence toward God

———

We are the circumcision, which worship
God in the spirit, and rejoice in Christ
Jesus, and have no confidence in the flesh.
– Philippians 3:3

It is not because of character that I, a sinner, can find favor in the eyes of God. Such is my character, even at its best, that I can base on it no plea of acceptance. I may labor hard to mend and improve it, yet after all, I find myself a sinner still. And being so, my character cannot justify me, nor can it in the very least contribute anything toward my justification.

I do not expect anything from God on account of what I am or feel or do. Granting that my character is a good one, still it is not so good that God can show me favor on account of it. I must therefore set it aside. I cannot act upon it or ask God to act upon it.

While my character, however good, cannot help me, still however bad, it cannot hinder me nor prevent my being received by God. What is good in me (if there is anything) does not make me better than a sinner, and what is bad does not make me worse. So that whatever I be, I must still meet God just as a sinner. And as such, He is willing to meet me; as such, He is willing to receive and bless me. The only condition He makes is that I come to Him as I am, making no secret of my sins nor pretending to be what I am not and never can be here – less than a sinner.

Day 52

The Justifying Thing

*The righteousness of God which is by faith
of Jesus Christ unto all and upon all them
that believe: for there is no difference.*
– Romans 3:22

I t is not on account of faith that we are justified, as
if by our act of believing we persuaded God to take
us into favor or as if there were anything of recommen-
datory or meritorious excellence in our faith. It is by or
through faith that we are justified; that is, by means of
the justifying object with which our faith connects us.

That justifying object is the righteousness of God's
incarnate Son. We are at once forgiven and accepted
when we are identified with the doing and the suffer-
ing of this righteous One, this Divine Substitute. That
which identifies us with these is our faith.

Thus, in the matter of justification we are simply
receivers, not givers nor workers. God presents to us the
righteousness of His Son, telling us that He is willing

to deal with us on the footing of that righteousness and that we are welcome to use it in coming to Him just as if it were our own. We take Him at His word, consent to be dealt with in this way, and employ the righteousness precisely as if it were our own. This is believing. This is how we are *justified by faith* (Romans 5:1) and why we are filled *with all joy and peace **in** believing, that ye may abound in hope, through the power of the Holy Ghost* (Romans 15:13).

The Justifying One

~

That He might be just, and the justifier of him which believeth in Jesus. It is God that justifieth.
– Romans 3:26; 8:33

He who has the right to condemn is the only one who has the right to justify. Only the Lawgiver can remit the penalty of the law and say to the transgressor, "You are justified from all things." And He has declared His purpose of doing so, and He has sent His Son to carry that purpose into effect by bearing *our sins in his own body on the tree* (1 Peter 2:24) so that God might be as just in forgiving as in condemning.

It is God that justifies! This assures us that justification is a certain thing, a thing that admits no doubt, and of which there can be no reversal. The sentence of acquittal from His lips is decisive and final. Our Judge and our Justifier are one.

And who are they whom He justifies? The ungodly.

To him that worketh not, but believeth on Him that justifieth the ungodly, his faith is counted for righteousness (Romans 4:5). It is not the good, the humble, the penitent, or the prayerful that He justifies. He justifies the ungodly. Then, being justified freely by His grace, they become good and humble and penitent and prayerful and holy.

Oh, it is folly without equal to wait until we are godly in order to be justified! It is a strange ignorance of the justifying work of the Divine Substitute to suppose that we need anything to qualify us for that work but our utter ungodliness!

The King in His Beauty

*Thou art fairer than the children of
men: grace is poured into thy lips: therefore God hath blessed thee for ever.*
– Psalm 45:2

The world is fair and bright. It has dazzled and ensnared millions. Yet there is such a thing as a newfound Savior, eclipsing and outshining all earthly beauty in the eyes even of those who once admired it most.

Every form of attraction gathers around Him. That attraction is resistless. With joyful swiftness, we hasten to Him whose wondrous goodliness we have newly discovered. We now move around Him as our center. We are drawn from vanities that once enchanted us. The world has lost its attractiveness; it has been utterly darkened. It shines no more. It wins no more. It is Egypt to us now, in which we were vile bondsmen. It is Babylon to us now, in which we were weary exiles and captives. But we are free. The true light has risen.

We have seen something that has drawn our eye and won our heart. The beauty of the world has vanished. Its luster has grown dim. In the love of Him who loved us and gave Himself for us, we have found that which has dissolved the bonds of earth and fastened us to heaven with an everlasting tie.

We have seen just a little of the glory, but it is enough to allure us away from vanity and to make us desire the day when we will see Him face to face, whom having not seen, we love (1 Peter 1:8).

Day 55

Divine Raiment

He hath covered me with the
robe of righteousness.
– Isaiah 61:10

Israel will sing this song in the latter day, when forgiven and restored, but meanwhile, the church can use it as her own. For hers, it has been said, is a robe "broad as the law, spotless as the light, and richer than an angel ever wore, the robe of Jesus." Jehovah Himself clothes her with it.

1. It is a robe of purity. There is not a stain on all its entire surface nor a blemish in any of its waving folds. Its purity is that of the sunbeam or the star beam, which nothing can soil or dim.

2. It is a robe of gladness. *Joy unspeakable and full of glory* (1 Peter 1:8) is woven into its texture, so that he who wears it cannot help but rejoice.

3. It is a robe of splendor. Its ornaments are the

jewels of a bride. It is the raiment of a queen. Its gems and its hues are all of heaven.

4. It is a robe of triumph. It is the festal dress – the robe that suits best the crown and the palm leaves which we are to wear in the kingdom.

5. It is a robe for eternity. It does not grow old. It does not fade. Ages do not dim its freshness nor antiquate its form. It is as incorruptible and imperishable as it is undefiled.

The clasp which fixes it around us is faith. In believing, we put it on and fasten it around us. In continuing to believe, we keep that robe around us, and we find in it sufficient covering even for deformities like ours. What storm of earth can unclasp it or tear it away?

Day 56

Forgiveness, the Root of Holiness

～

He shall put his hand upon the head of
the burnt-offering; and it shall be accepted
for him to make atonement for him.
– Leviticus 1:4

My person must be accepted before any of my doings can be. The worshipper must be accepted before his worship can be acceptable.

This is the answer to those who think to secure acceptance by labor, penance, self-denial, good deeds, or prayers. Their efforts are fruitless. No, they are worse; they invert God's order and subvert the foundation that He has laid. He has said that the person must be accepted before the work, and He has made full provision of everything needed for our acceptance, so that nothing remains for us to do in order to secure but to simply recognize the completeness of that provision and avail ourselves of it in drawing near to God.

The moment that I receive God's testimony to His

Son and to His work as the sinner's substitute, I am accepted, and from then on an acceptable worshipper and a successful laborer for God. Until I believe, I am not accepted in person, for I am refusing to acknowledge Him in whom God is well pleased. Neither can any of my works find favor with God. How necessary, then, that we should understand the right beginning, lest we grope on in bondage and darkness all our days! We begin by simply believing, and in that way, we go on unto the end, complete in Christ and accepted through Him before the Father.

What Is the Depth of
Your Religion?

—⁓—

*I ate no pleasant bread, neither came
flesh nor wine in my mouth.*
– Daniel 10:3

Many years ago, a man of God, David Brainerd, wrote in his diary: "I was enabled to persevere in prayer until I saw so much need of divine help that I knew not how to stop and had forgotten that I needed food."

Strange intensity of desire! He must have been far above most Christians of our age. Who of us could record the same longings of his soul?

We feel that this is reality. There is no insobriety or wild excitement here. All is calm and deep. We are listening to the utterances of a soul that has gotten into conscious contact and vital fellowship with God, and who, in the profound enjoyment entered on, has lost the consciousness of this outer world in which he is still a dweller.

Happy saint! Who would not tread your footsteps and get as completely within the veil as you! All your religion was amid realities and certainties. There was no distance, no dimness, no vagueness in your connection with the Father of spirits. How much of our religion is made up of shadows and incoherencies! How much of our relationship with God is vague and distant; a groping after something which we seem never to reach instead of being living, personal, conscious communication between our souls and God!

Live for Something

⌁

See then that ye walk circumspectly,
not as fools, but as wise, redeeming
the time, because the days are evil.
– Ephesians 5:15-16

O ur life here as saints is no aimless life. We know
the true way of living. We have found an object
worthy of our living for. In all we speak and do, we
serve the Lord Christ.

We do not live at random. Each hour, each word,
each action, has its aim. We come far short of that which
we propose to ourselves, but we still have always something in our view – something exalted, large, unselfish.
Something that will last for eternity.

We have finished with idleness, frivolity, and vain
amusement. Our desire is not to kill time, but to use it;
to gather up all its fragments, to lay out every moment
well, to lose nothing of so precious a boon. All that we

have of it is too little to be trifled with, too precious to be thrown away.

We want to live active lives. We cannot afford to be idle; neither do we desire it. The call is, *Redeem the time.* Be always doing something that will last. Always stretch forward to the prize. It will soon be ours, for the Lord is coming soon. It is a prize worth all our labor and sorrow here. The very thought of it is enough to put to flight all murmuring, selfishness, or sloth. To labor here is as blessed as it is to rest hereafter. Work on, work on, until the day of recompense arrives.

Day 59

Spend and Be Spent

⁓

Be instant in season, out of season.
– 2 Timothy 4:2

"I confess," says Richard Baxter, "to my shame, that I remember no one sin that my conscience so much accuses and judges me for as doing so little for the saving of men's souls and dealing no more fervently and earnestly with them for their conversion. I confess to you that when I am alone and think of the condition of poor, ignorant, worldly, earthly, unconverted sinners that live not for God nor set their hearts on the life to come, my conscience tells me that I should go to as many as I can and tell them plainly and roundly what will become of them if they do not turn, and to beseech them, with all the earnestness that I can, to come in to Christ and make no delay. And though I have many excuses coming from other business and from disability and lack of time, none of them satisfies my own conscience when I consider what heaven and hell are, which will, one of them, be the end of every man's life. My conscience tells me that I should follow them with all possible earnestness, night and day, taking no denial of them until they return to God."

Our land would be so much better if each minister were like Baxter! Better still if each Christian were like him! But where are such ministers, where are such Christians to be found? The time is short. People are dying. The night comes. Let us hurry if we desire to do anything for a perishing world.

Day 60

Stand Fast

———

Stand fast in the faith, quit
you like men, be strong.
– 1 Corinthians 16:13

I n the last days, many will be as *wells without water,*
clouds that are carried with a tempest (2 Peter 2:17).
And this is one of the special perils of these *perilous*
times (2 Timothy 3:1). The winds are let loose and are
now performing their awful work of tossing hither and
thither these empty clouds.

Consequently, instability prevails. Men are *carried*
about with every wind of doctrine (Ephesians 4:14). They
are not *rooted and grounded in love* (Ephesians 3:17), and
having never *tasted that the Lord is gracious* (1 Peter 2:3)
nor rested their weary souls upon Him, they go around
looking for something, but they do not know what.
They want something that will fill them, but not going
to the divine fulness of the incarnate Word for it, they
wander on in sadness of spirit, vainly trying to soothe

119

their uneasy souls with every new doctrine or device that meets them in the way! All in vain. For what can be a substitute for God and His free love?

Amid all this instability, let us *stand fast in the faith*. Let us be *strong in the grace that is in Christ Jesus* (2 Timothy 2:1). Let us beware of novelties in religion. Let us guard against fickleness of opinion and hastiness in decision. Satan will let loose his blasts and call up his storms; let us moor our vessel firmer and keep a stronger hold of the anchor, which is *sure and stedfast, and which entereth into that within the veil* (Hebrews 6:19). This way, in patience we will possess our souls, for *he that believeth shall not make haste* (Isaiah 28:16).

Watch

~

Watch therefore: for ye know not
what hour your Lord doth come.
– Matthew 24:42

The Lord is coming soon! The world's Judge and King will soon be here. Is this not a rousing, quickening word? And seeing that it is so, may we not say to one and to all, *Watch*?

He comes suddenly and swiftly as the lightning flashing out from the sky and bursting down on the earth in a moment. Therefore, watch.

He comes silently and stealthily as the thief coming in at midnight on a slumbering house, without note of warning. Therefore, watch.

He comes as a snare, which the fowler casts noiselessly over his prey to entangle and seize it before it is aware. Therefore, watch.

He comes to raise His dead saints and to change His living ones. He comes to execute vengeance upon those that do not know God or obey His gospel (Psalm 149:7). He comes to smite the nations in His wrath and to kindle a fire in His anger. He comes to bind Satan, to destroy Antichrist, to set up His kingdom, to dispel the long darkness of earth, and to bring in the long-promised day. Watch, therefore, and be ready!

What if He should now be on His way, and what if this uproar of the nations be the sound of His chariot wheels? The night is almost over, the day is nearly here. Let us sleep no more. Let us get up and be serious, for the time that remains is short.

Day 62

Surely, I Come Quickly

—〜—

He which testifieth these things
saith, Surely I come quickly. Amen.
Even so, come, Lord Jesus.
– Revelation 22:20

The Lord did not mean these words to be empty sounds. He meant His church to listen and pay attention to the solemn announcement. They speak to each passing age with a deeper tone and a more rousing voice. The voice of this trumpet grows louder and louder as the ages roll away.

Now is our salvation nearer than when we believed (Romans 13:11). Are we, in the eager joy of our hearts, trying to measure the ages and count the few years or days that may lie between us and the Lord? Who would be surprised if we did? Who would not wonder if we did not?

His wife hath made herself ready (Revelation 19:7). Are we ready? Is the bridal dress put on, the *fine linen, clean and white* (Revelation 19:8)? Are we dressed up for the marriage supper? Are we keeping our garments undefiled? Are we keeping ourselves *in the love of God, looking for the mercy of our Lord Jesus Christ unto eternal life* (Jude 21)?

And are we warning the ungodly? Are we Noahs in the prospect of that fiery deluge that is coming on the earth? Are we preachers of righteousness (2 Peter 2:5)? Do we condemn the world (Hebrews 11:7)? Are we laboring to pluck brands from the burning (Zechariah 3:2)? Are we becoming more and more earnest in urging our message upon sinners? *Flee from the wrath to come!*

Horatius Bonar
A Brief Biography

Born on December 19, 1808, Horatius Bonar was one of eleven children of James Bonar and Marjory Pyott Maitland Bonar. For several generations his ancestors had been ministers of the gospel.

Bonar graduated from the University of Edinburgh where Dr. Thomas Chalmers laid the foundation for solid learning, which continued through the years. This gave Bonar direction and strength during his most impressionable years. He was ordained in 1838 and accepted North Parish, Kelso, as his first parish.

In addition to Dr. Chalmers, he allied himself with William C. Burns and Robert Murray McCheyne as spiritual mentors and friends.

As a young pastor, Bonar preached in villages and farmhouses throughout his district, for he saw evangelization in a different light from his other contemporaries. To him, Christ had to come first, not numbers of converts. In his house-to-house visitation, he proved himself as a comforter of the sorrowful and a guide for the confused. Colossians 3:23 was the verse he lived by: *Whatsoever ye do, do it heartily, as to the Lord, and not unto men.*

In 1843, he joined the Free Church of Scotland after the "Disruption." The old church with its civil service pastors had failed to arouse the faith of the nation. This disruption was a schism in the Church of Scotland where about 450 evangelical ministers broke away over an issue of the church's relationship with the state. There was disagreement about whether the church was sovereign within its own domain with Christ as Head or if the king was head. In this way, it was similar to the Lutheran Reformation.

Those who left forfeited their livelihood, pulpits, and aid from the established church to found and finance a new national church from scratch. They needed to train clergy and form a new college, which opened in 1843, with Dr. Chalmers as the first principal. Most of the protest principles were conceded by Parliament by 1929, which paved the way for reunification.

In 1843, Horatius Bonar married Jane Catharine Lundie. Together they had nine children, but five of them died before adulthood – three in infancy. One surviving daughter was later widowed with five children, so she moved back with her parents. Horatius said, "God took five children from life some years ago, and He has given me another five to bring up for Him in my old age."

In 1851, he wrote *Man: His Religion and His World* because he was concerned that pastors were diluting the gospel to make it pleasant and easier to accept. He always contended for the truth and never neglected pastoral work and preaching.

Horatius Bonar received an honorary degree of Doctor of Divinity from the University of Aberdeen and then visited Palestine on a mission to the Jews in 1856, which gave him the inspiration for the hymn "The Voice from Galilee," better known as "I Heard the Voice of Jesus Say." Revival had sprung up in Scotland while he was away, and he came back with a renewed interest in prophecy and a firm belief in the personal coming and reign of Jesus Christ. He did not believe that the world was getting better and civilization could save the world. Teachings of the coming of Christ, the tribulation, and the thousand-year reign had been lost, and the nineteenth-century preachers had to bring these doctrines back.

Bonar spoke as a dying man to dying men, resulting in many conversions. He wrote the *Kelso Tracts* to warn the careless, to present salvation simply, and to edify the saints. The tracts had wide circulation in Scotland, England, and America. In 1867, Bonar moved to Edinburgh to take over Chalmers' Memorial Church, and in 1883, he was elected moderator of the General

Assembly of the Free Church of Scotland. Bonar continued to express his views in *Prophetical Landmarks* (1847) and served as editor of *The Quarterly Journal of Prophecy* (1848-1873) and the *Christian Treasury* (1859-1879). He even wrote biographies of ministers like *The Life of the Rev. John Milne of Perth* and *The Life and Works of the Rev. G. T. Dodds.*

Other books and tracts that bear his name are *Night of Weeping*, *The Everlasting Righteousness*, and *How Shall I Go to God?* Until his death, he warned about trends he saw creeping in and threatening the Christian church. In one of his last books – *Our Ministry: How It Touches the Questions of the Age* – he observed that "Man is now thinking out a Bible for himself, framing a religion in harmony with the development of liberal thought, constructing a worship on the principles of taste and culture, and shaping a God to suit the expanding aspirations of the age."

Horatius Bonar is best known as the principle hymn writer of Scotland. He was called the "prince of Scottish hymn writers." As he worked with young people, he realized they lacked enthusiasm. Even though he lacked an ear for music, he knew familiar tunes and wrote new words to them for the children. His experiment worked and the children became interested in the verses that were written for them personally. Because they were full of sound teaching, many adults loved to sing them also and requested to use them in other churches. He always granted permission for any church to use his hymns as long as they did not change his words.

He wrote more than six hundred hymns, and many

hymnbooks carry these songs. Several are completely compiled from his hymns. The three volumes of *Hymns of Faith and Hope* contain a multitude of his hymns. While "I Heard the Voice of Jesus Say" and "My Redeemer Liveth" were two of the best known, he is largely remembered for his hymns that were based strongly on theology and doctrine, such as "Done is the Work That Saves" and "No Blood, No Altar Now." He wrote of justification, sanctification, the second coming, and the exaltation of Christ.

His hymns are childlike yet manly, hopeful but sympathetic. For many years they were mostly used by churches of other denominations but not his own. The Free Church of Scotland was opposed to singing at worship anything but metrical psalms and paraphrases.

Bonar believed "life is a journey, not a home; a road, not a city of habitation." He stated that "It is not the opinions that man needs; it is truth. It is not theology; it is God. It is not religion; it is Christ. It is not literature and science; but the knowledge of the free love of God in the gift of His only begotten Son." From the first day of his ministry until his last sermon, he closed with these words: "In such an hour as ye think not, the Son of Man cometh."

Other Similar Titles

The Night of Weeping,
by Horatius Bonar

It was God's purpose from the beginning not merely to redeem sinners from His condemnation but also to bring those people into a special relationship with Himself. It is His desire to draw mankind closer to Himself than any other of His creatures and to establish a most special link between His people and Himself.

Since we know that God has our best intentions in mind, what should move us? What can ruin our joy? Our rejoicing is in the Lord, and He is good and has good plans for us. We know that this current life is not our rest, nor do we wish it were, for it is polluted; but our joy is this, that Jehovah is our God, and His promised glory is our inheritance forever. We are being molded and shaped into a vessel fit for His Kingdom!

Available where books are sold.

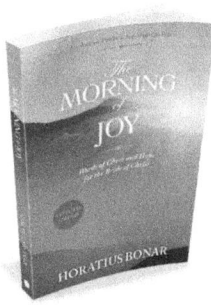

The Morning of Joy
by Horatius Bonar

Stars may help to make the sky less gloomy, but they are not the sun – and besides, clouds have now covered them so they are no longer visible. Torches and beacon lights do not help. Our own lights make no impression upon the darkness; it is so deep, so real, so unmistakable. We might give up all for lost if we were not assured that there is a sun and that it is hastening to rise, and we are watching for it.

The church's pilgrimage is nearly complete, yet she is no less a pilgrim as its end draws near. The last stage of the journey might be the dreariest for her. Her path lies through the thickest darkness that the world has yet felt. It is the sound of falling kingdoms that is guiding us onward. It is the fragments of broken thrones lying across our path that assure us that our route is the true one and that its end is near. Then comes the morning with its songs; and in that morning, a kingdom; and in that kingdom, glory; and in that glory, the everlasting rest, the Sabbath of eternity.

Available where books are sold.

Follow the Lamb
by Horatius Bonar

Your "turning" or "conversion" is only a beginning, and no more. It is not the whole journey; it is merely the first step. You are a disciple, that is, one who is under teaching; but your teaching, your discipleship, has only *just begun.* Your life is a book; it may be a bigger or smaller volume, but conversion is only the title page or the preface. The book itself remains to be written, and your years, weeks, and days are its chapters, pages, and lines. It is a book written for eternity; make sure that it is written well. It is a book for the inspection of enemies as well as friends; be careful of every word. It is a book written under the eye of God; let it be done reverently, not frivolously, but also without constraint or terror.

Available where books are sold.